AnimalWays

Owls

AnimalWays

Owls

Tom Warhol

Marshall Cavendish
Benchmark
New York

With thanks to Dr. Dan Wharton, director of the Central Park Wildlife
Center, for his expert reading of this manuscript.

Marshall Cavendish Benchmark
99 White Plains Road
Tarrytown, NY 10591
www.marshallcavendish.us

Library of Congress Cataloging-in-Publication Data

Warhol, Tom.
Owls / by Tom Warhol.
p. cm. — (Animals ways)
Summary: "Describes the physical characteristics, habitat, behavior, diet,
life cycle, and conservation status of owls"—Provided by publisher.
Includes bibliographical references and index.
ISBN-13: 978-0-7614-2537-3
1. Owls—Juvenile literature. I. Title. II. Series.
QL696.S8W284 2007
598.9'7—dc22
2006019708

Photo research by Candlepants Incorporated

Cover photo: Purestock / SuperStock

The photographs in this book are used by permission and through the courtesy of:
Minden Pictures: Korad Wothe, 2; Tom Vezo, 37, 77; Rob Reijnen/Foto Natura, 41; Tim
Fitzharris, 43; Jan Van Arkel/Foto Natura, 58; Michael Durham, 63; FransLanting, 64, 95;
Bert Muller/Foto Natura, 73; Mark Moffett, 91; Michio Hoshino, 96. Corbis: Gary W.
Carter, 9; Gunter Marx Photography, 16; Clem Haagner, Gallo Images, 21; W. Perry
Conway, 28; Joe McDonald, 31; Herbert Kehrer/zefa, 34; Kevin Schafer, 38; Manfred
Danegger/zefa, 47; Peter Reynolds, Frank Lane Picture Agency, 60; George McCarthy, 74;
Jim Richardson, 99. SuperStock: James Urbach, 11; Mauritius, 25; age fotostock, 45, 66,
68, 71, 80, 85, 101, back cover; David W. Middleton, 89. *Art Resource, NY*: Erich Lessing,
14. Photo Researchers Inc.: Chris Butler, 19; Simon Fraser, 33; Anthony Mercieca, 40;
Tierbild Okapia, 53; Paal Hermansen, 82. Peter Arnold Inc.: Klein, 22, 79; Harvey, 50; S. J.
Krasemann, 55; Tom Vezo, 103; Hans Pfletschinger, 86.

Publisher: Michelle Bisson
Art Director: Anahid Hamparian

Printed in Malaysia
1 3 5 6 4 2

Contents

HERE ARE SOME OF THE MAIN PHYLA, CLASSES, AND ORDERS, WITH PHOTOGRAPHS OF A TYPICAL ANIMAL FROM EACH GROUP.

Animal Kingdom

CNIDARIANS

coral

ARTHROPODS
(animals with jointed limbs and external skeleton)

MOLLUSKS

squid

CRUSTACEANS

crab

ARACHNIDS

spider

INSECTS

grasshopper

MYRIAPODS

centipede

CARNIVORES

lion

SEA MAMMALS

whale

PRIMATES

orangutan

HERBIVORES
(5 orders)

elephant

PHYLA

ANNELIDS

earthworm

CHORDATES
(animals with a dorsal nerve chord)

ECHINODERMS

starfish

SUB PHYLA

VERTEBRATES
(animals with a backbone)

CLASSES

FISH

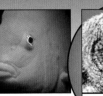

fish

BIRDS

OWLS

MAMMALS

AMPHIBIANS

frog

REPTILES

snake

ORDERS

RODENTS

squirrel

INSECTIVORES

mole

MARSUPIALS

koala

SMALL MAMMALS
(several orders)

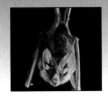

bat

1 Owl Lore and Legend

As the last rays of sunlight seep out of the forest, the buzz of insects and the calls of songbirds drift away with them. Dusk fills in the details with shadows, and the trees are now only silhouettes against the western sky. The songbirds settle onto their nighttime roosts as the late shift clocks in. Nocturnal (which means "active at night") creatures awaken and begin their hunt for food. Raccoons and opossums scramble out of their burrows or tree holes; bats take flight from their roosts in caves and trees, fanning out to feast on the bountiful crop of insects; and the repetitive chirping of mating frogs echoes throughout the forest.

Suddenly this chatter is broken by a haunting sound—a deep, sonorous hooting. The barred owl stirs, stretching its wings and legs. Shaking its body and fluffing its feathers, the owl spreads its wings and drops from its perch, nimbly making its way through the maze of trees and shrubs until it arrives at a wet meadow. Alighting on a branch in a tree at the edge of the meadow, the night hunter settles on its perch, listening and watching.

BARRED OWLS MAKE THEIR HOMES IN MATURE FORESTS OF THE EASTERN UNITED STATES AND SOUTHERN CANADA. THE OLDER, LARGER TREES PROVIDE LIMBS FOR PERCHING, COVER FOR DAYTIME ROOSTING, AND NESTING HOLES FOR RAISING YOUNG.

It is almost fully dark now, but the barred owl can still see movement among the grasses. With its sensitive hearing, it detects the high-pitched squeaks and rustlings of the various rodents—voles, mice, muskrats—that are searching for seeds, nuts, and grasses to eat. The owl swivels its head around, while tipping it to the side, before bobbing it from side to side and up and down. By doing this, it swiftly locates the exact source of the sounds—a vole rustling in the grasses behind a log at the edge of the stream.

Spreading its wings, the owl drops from its perch, swooping low to avoid detection, although it hardly needs to, since the vole doesn't see nearly as well in the dark as the owl. In addition, the barred owl's feathers are designed to muffle the sound of the air, so that the approach of the large bird is silent.

The owl dives straight toward the vole and then, at the last second, pulls its wings back and thrusts its powerful, sharp talons forward, spreading them wide at first, then closing them tightly around the vole's body before the rodent can even look up from its foraging. When the vole stops wriggling, the owl bends low and crushes the rodent's skull with its beak. Seconds after the kill, the owl is back on a nearby perch. Standing atop its prey, the first of the night, the owl tears the vole apart with its sharp beak.

Owl Basics

Owls are among the top predators of the nighttime world. They have large round heads that can revolve three-quarters of the way around their bodies. Their large, forward-facing, highly sensitive eyes are set within a facial ruff, or disk, of short feathers that serves to focus sounds on their extremely receptive ears. The "ear tufts" on top of the heads of some owl species are not ears at all, and they have nothing to do with hearing. They are merely longer feathers that might be useful for communication or as camouflage (to help them blend in with their surroundings). These ear tufts can look like the broken ends of branches, and their plumage, or coat of feathers, often mimics the colors and patterns of their roosting places, such as trees or grasses.

Owls' nocturnal habits and effective camouflage—in the form of their plumage—make them mysterious creatures, rarely seen. But their calls and songs—hoots, shrieks, whinnies, and

GREAT GRAY OWLS HAVE RELATIVELY SMALL EYES IN LARGE FACIAL DISKS, BOTH INDICATIONS THAT THIS OWL SPECIES USES HEARING MORE THAN EYESIGHT WHEN HUNTING.

other cries—make them well-known and feared presences in woodlands, grasslands, and even graveyards.

Not all owls are nocturnal. Some are crepuscular, meaning they are most active at dawn and dusk. Others, such as short-eared owls, are diurnal—active during the day. Like most owls that live in the far north, where the sun doesn't set during the summer, snowy owls and great gray owls have no choice but to be active in the daytime.

Owls are predators. Larger species, such as great-horned owls and barred owls, prefer rodents and other mammals. The tawny owl has one of the most varied diets: large insects, frogs, songbirds, ducks, other owls, and rabbits. Smaller owls, such as pygmy and elf owls, are insectivorous, meaning they eat mostly insects.

Wise Old Owls

A myth told by the Cherokees of North America describes how owls became creatures of the night. After all the animals were made, the creator told them to stay awake for seven days. As the days passed, more and more animals fell asleep, until only the owl and the cougar were left awake. The creator gave these creatures the power to see in the dark and, since then, they have hunted by night.

From the beginnings of human civilization, owls have been prominent figures in the stories and legends of many cultures. Owls were considered to be wise because of their seemingly calm appearance, sitting on a perch patiently watching and waiting. Their nocturnal behavior was also like that of dedicated scholars who worked long into the night.

Their place in today's literature, from *Winnie the Pooh* to the Harry Potter books, has grown from these ancient associations.

Merlin, sorcerer companion of King Arthur, often had a talking barn owl named Archimedes on his shoulder. In *The Book of Merlyn,* by T. H. White, the owl was a member of the group of animals called together to instruct the king.

One of the earliest known representations of owls is a rock painting in France, dating from more than 30,000 years ago. Other early paintings of owls from ancient cultures have been found in Australia and in Washington State in the United States.

In Mesopotamia, owls were believed to be the companions of Lilith, the goddess of death. This mythological figure was probably the inspiration for the Greek goddess Athena, whose role as the wise warrior was associated with owls as well. The little owl's scientific name, *Athene noctua,* was inspired by Athena.

Like the gods and goddesses of most peoples conquered by the Roman Empire, Athena was incorporated into Roman beliefs. Her name was changed to Minerva, the goddess who could predict the future.

In many other cultures, owls were also considered symbols of power and luck. In North America, mighty Oglala Sioux warriors wore snowy owl feather caps to symbolize their bravery. The owl was an emblem of protection for the Pawnee as well. Tlingit warriors hooted like owls to prepare for battle as well as to scare their enemies. The Zuni tell a story of the burrowing owl, called the priest of the prairie dogs, who helped drive the storm clouds away.

One Algonquin story tells of the time when men and animals spoke the same language and lived together in peace. When this peace was shattered by their eventual arguing, the Great Spirit Glooskap left this world, disgusted by their behavior. All the men and animals mourned. That is why every night the snowy owl wanders the great north woods, calling and calling, "*koo, koo, koo*" ("Oh, I am sorry. Oh, I am sorry.") until Glooskap returns.

The Ainu, native peoples of Hokkaido, Japan, honored Blakiston's fish owl, known to them as Kotan Kor Kamur, meaning "god of the village." The owl is seen as a protective figure by the Ainu, who use carved figurines of the eagle owl in their homes to keep away sickness and famine. In the Aboriginal cultures of southern Australia, owls were honored and protected

THE LITTLE OWL WAS THE SYMBOL OF ATHENA, GREEK GODDESS OF WISDOM AND WARFARE, AND WAS PROTECTED IN AND AROUND GREEK CITIES AND TOWNS. THIS BIRD EVEN APPEARED ON GREEK COINS.

because they represented the souls of women, while bats represented the souls of men.

The Tartars of Russia long respected owls because Genghis Khan, their great leader, was saved by one. After a fierce, hard-fought battle, Khan and his men fled the battlefield and hid beneath a tree. An owl landed in the branches above. When the enemy forces came upon the tree, they avoided it because they feared the bird. Tartars wore owl plumes on their heads from that point on.

Soul Bearers

Since owls are creatures of the night, their habits were not well known by many early peoples (and are still not fully understood today). Most often owls could be heard but not seen. Their various and often unnerving nighttime calls have sent chills down people's spines since the early days of humans.

Some believed that when a person died, his or her soul was linked to an owl that carried it into the afterlife. Many Native American cultures held similar beliefs, so owls were respected figures, not to be harmed. Shamans, or spiritual leaders, believed owls showed them connections to the supernatural world.

But owls' association with the night, their predatory habits, and their haunting calls have also prompted fear in people. While to some they represented wisdom, luck, and fertility, many others believed owls signified bad omens, misfortune, and death.

Unlike Athena's wise owl, in ancient Rome, the goddess Minerva's owl eventually became a symbol of evil, a bearer of bad news. *Striges,* the root of Strigiformes—the Latin name for the owl group—was the Roman word for "witch." Dead owls were nailed to doors to ward off evil and bad weather from Roman times up until the nineteenth century in England.

OWLS WERE VERY IMPORTANT AND RESPECTED CREATURES IN MANY NATIVE
AMERICAN CULTURES, INCLUDING THE GITXSAN TRIBES OF BRITISH COLUMBIA, WHOSE
MEMBERS CARVED THIS OWL FIGURE INTO THEIR TOTEM POLE.

The owl's association with death has its roots in many cultures, including those of Europe, Egypt, Japan, China, and India. These beliefs may have come about because owls were often found near cemeteries and sacred sites. In many places near towns and cities in India, the largest trees are often found in cemeteries, and these are the perfect places for owls, which nest in holes in large trees. When people heard the owls' calls coming from these places, they believed that these birds were carrying off the spirits of the dead.

Mictlantecutli, the ruler of Mictlan, the Aztec realm of the dead, was depicted as an owl grasping a skull and crossbones. Some European cultures believed that if an owl was heard calling around a house, the occupant would soon die. To the Oto of Missouri, an owl's hooting is a death warning. In some parts of Africa, owls are also considered evil.

Many poems throughout history describe owls as symbols of death. William Shakespeare described the owl as "the fatal bellman which gives the stern'st goodnight."

Even more modern cultures still believe superstitions about owls. Cajuns of Louisiana will turn a shoe over or turn their shirt inside out when they hear an owl calling, in the hope that the owl will stop its hooting and any bad luck will be avoided.

2 Evolution

Just as owls have inspired a long list of folktales and cultural associations, their fossil record is even longer, possibly one of the longest of all living bird groups.

Early Owls

Birds originally evolved from a group of dinosaurs called theropods. One of the first birds, *Archaeopteryx,* was alive 140 million years ago and has long since died out. But from that ancient bird, most, if not all, of today's bird groups evolved.

As those birds spread throughout the world, they became more specialized, adapting to different habitats (natural environments) and seeking out a variety of food sources. They became increasingly isolated from their relatives, and over a long period of time they developed behaviors and anatomies specific to their new lives. This is how new species form, part of a process called speciation.

The evolution of owls as a distinct group began when they split off from another group of birds known as nightjars about 70 to 80 million years ago. Like owls, nightjars are nocturnal predators, but they feed mostly on insects.

ARCHAEOPTERYX WAS THE FIRST FEATHERED DINOSAUR FOUND TO SHOW THE FOSSIL LINK BETWEEN REPTILES AND BIRDS. THE ANIMAL'S SKELETAL STRUCTURE, CLAWS, AND OTHER FEATURES DISPLAY CHARACTERISTICS OF BOTH ANIMAL GROUPS.

The earliest known owl was *Ogygoptynx*, a distinctive bird from North America that appeared in the early Paleocene epoch, about 54 to 65 million years ago. This was a period when much of the world was warmer and more humid than it is today. Most of the plants were conifers, evergreen trees with needlelike leaves and cones. There were few trees with flowers.

The earliest fossils of modern owls appeared in France and date to the Oligocene epoch, which lasted from about 24 to 36 million years ago. Modern owls evolved from these early ancestors. Barn owls, Tytonidae, appeared first in the fossil record. True owls, Strigidae, appeared later in the Miocene epoch around 22 to 24 million years ago.

The Night Hawks

While owls were evolving their predatory traits, another group of birds—hawks—was doing the same. Despite their similarities—sharp, pointed beaks; powerful feet and talons; excellent eyesight; similar prey—hawks and owls are not directly related. This type of species development is called parallel evolution: two unrelated groups develop the same traits because of environmental conditions.

Owls and hawks have evolved other similar traits. Owls and falcons, a subgroup of hawks, both kill their prey in the same way, by snapping its neck with their beaks. Unlike other birds of prey, neither owls nor falcons build nests; depending on the species, they either use nests built by other birds or they use a shallow hole in the ground. Owls and hawks are mostly monogamous, meaning they often mate for life, and the males of both groups provide the food for the hatchlings while the female stays at the nest, protecting the hatchlings and keeping them warm. Female owls and hawks are larger than males, an adaptation

HAWKS AND OWLS PLAY THE SAME ECOLOGICAL ROLE—WINGED PREDATORS—AND
HAVE SIMILAR TRAITS, BUT THESE TWO FAMILIES EVOLVED SEPARATELY.

The evolution of rodents, like this mouse, and flowering and fruiting plants paved the way for predators like owls to evolve and develop.

unusual among birds. Finally, both owls and hawks regurgitate pellets, plugs of undigested hair, feathers, bones, and exoskeletons (the outer casings of insects).

Owls and hawks rely on sight to find their food, but owls also depend on highly evolved hearing, a necessary tool for creatures that hunt at night. Since these two groups lived in the same territory, they eventually shifted their hunting times to different parts of the day to avoid competition. Modern species still take shifts. Great horned owls, a species of eagle owl native to North America, often hunt the same territories at night that red-tailed hawks hunt during the day, although the animals that the two birds of prey feed on may be different.

Owls and Flowers

As with all birds, owls really began to develop and evolve into distinct species after flowering plants became widespread in the late Cretaceous and early Tertiary periods. The development of these plants caused a dramatic change in practically all life on Earth. Flowering plants provided the world with edible seeds, often contained in tasty fruits. This abundance of new food aided the development of large numbers of small mammals, namely rodents, who fed on the fruits and seeds.

Rodents were, and still are, remarkably successful creatures; they established themselves in nearly every habitat in the world. Today there are about 1,500 species of rodents. The rodents themselves became a valuable food source for a growing group of carnivorous mammals that included wolves, cats, and birds of prey. The rodents learned to be alert and inconspicuous, qualities they needed to survive this wealth of predators.

In this way the emergence of flowering plants began what is called the age of mammals. The development of this food chain spurred the evolution of the birds that became today's owls.

3 Owls of the World

Mostly nocturnal, owls are not easily seen as they go about their lives, but they are out there, hunting prey that ranges from insects to rabbits. Owls can be observed during the day, but only if they are startled from their roosts. They blend in and hide themselves well, sticking close to a tree trunk, for example, that in many cases matches the color and pattern of their feathers.

Owls occupy many different habitats—desert, tundra, forest, grassland—and all continents, except Antarctica. They come in all shapes and sizes, from the tiny 5-inch (12.7-centimeter), 1.3-ounce (36.9-gram) elf owl to the Eurasian eagle owl, which can measure up to 28 inches (71.1 cm) and weigh up to 9 pounds (4 kilograms).

Like all life on Earth, owls are classified according to a binomial (meaning "two-name") system based on the Latin language. These Latin names are the best way for scientists to refer to these species because the same bird may be known by

THE COLOR AND ARRANGEMENT OF OWLS' PLUMAGE HELP THEM TO BLEND IN WITH THEIR ENVIRONMENT. THIS OWL LOOKS JUST LIKE THE BARK OF THE TREE IN WHICH IT IS ROOSTING.

varying common names in different parts of its range. For example, the snowy owl is also known by other common names, including the arctic owl and the white owl. But this bird has only one Latin name: *Bubo scandiacus*—first its genus name, then its species name. Domain names are the broadest level of classification, while species names are the narrowest and most specific means of defining life.

Owls are in the order Strigiformes, which is divided into two families. The Tytonidae family includes all the barn and grass owls and the bay owl. The Strigidae, or true owl, family includes all other genera (the plural of genus): screech and scops owls, eagle owls, wood and spectacled owls, pygmy owls, the elf owl, eared owls, little owls, forest owls, and hawk owls. These two families comprise the 26 genera and 212 species of owls.

This table shows how the barn owl, in the Tytonidae family, and the great horned owl, in the Strigidae family, are classified:

	Barn owl	Great horned owl
Domain	Eucarya	Eucarya
Kingdom	Animalia	Animalia
Phylum	Chordata	Chordata
Class	Aves	Aves
Order	Strigiformes	Strigiformes
Family	Tytonidae	Strigidae
Genus	*Tyto*	*Bubo*
Species	*alba*	*virginianus*

Owls have traditionally been classified by their physical appearance, especially the structure of their ears. But scientists are discovering that one of owls' most distinctive behavioral traits, their songs and calls, can be used to help identify and classify their different species as well.

Owl Families

Barn, Bay, and Grass Owls (Tytonidae).

There are about eighteen species within this family. These owls have well-developed facial disks and, consequently, exceptional hearing. The Tytonidae also have smaller eyes than most owls, because they rely more on sound than on sight when hunting.

The owls in this group range from 11 to 21 inches (27.9 to 53.3 cm) in length and have long wings, short tails, long legs, and no ear tufts. The single species of bay owl is unusual for this family, with its short, rounded wings and less complete facial disk. The grass owls' long, mostly unfeathered legs are ideal for running along the ground and catching prey hiding in dense grass. These unusual owls nest on the ground on a bed of trampled vegetation.

The Tytonidae can be found in North and South America, Europe, most of Africa, southern Asia, and Australia. The best known and most widely distributed example of this group is the barn owl. Its territories include forest edges and open habitats near human settlements, where small rodents—the owl's main prey—are readily found. Churches, barns, and ruins, as well as cliffs, holes in trees, and caves, all serve as roosts for these silent nighttime hunters.

The light brown upper body, the white heart-shaped facial disk, and the white underbody lend these birds a ghostly appearance when they swoop down on their outspread wings along the edge of a field on a moonlit night. Their call is a long, harsh screech.

ANIMALS OWLS PREY ON, SUCH AS MICE AND RATS, LIVE IN AND AROUND FARMS AND TOWNS. THUS, BARN OWLS CAN OFTEN BE CLOSE TO HUMAN SETTLEMENTS.

The central toe on each of a barn owl's feet has a distinctly jagged inner edge. It uses this for grooming the feathers on its head.

The wingspan of a barn owl can reach 38 inches (96.5 cm) and the body 13 inches (33 cm) from the head to the tip of the tail. Females are slightly larger than males. Barn owls' weights vary, depending on the population. Eurasian birds on average weigh 11 ounces (311.9 g) for males and 14 ounces (397 g) for females, although North American populations average 15.4 ounces (440 g) for males and 17.2 ounces (490 g) for females. Because barn owls have established themselves over a wide range, roughly thirty subspecies have developed.

The smallest member of this family, the bay owl, is very different from the barn owl. Bay owls are only 9 to 13 inches (22.9 to 33 cm) long and weigh just 9 to 11 ounces (255.2 to 311.9 g). Their facial disks are divided in half by a V-shaped shield of short feathers and hold larger eyes than those of barn owls. The bay owl also uses complex songs and calls, which include a series of rising and falling whistles. The dense forests of Southeast Asia are the bay owl's home. It hunts near water, catching small rodents, birds, bats, reptiles, and insects. Although this species is hard to find and difficult to study, scientists still believe they know enough about the population to consider it rare.

True Owls (Strigidae)

Screech and Scops Owls. The sixty-seven species of screech and scops owls are mostly small, with prominent ear tufts and short, rounded wings. These owls have less pronounced facial disks than barn owls do. Most species have bright yellow eyes. Their plumage can occur in two different colors, rufous (rusty red) and gray. The gray owls usually make their daytime roosts at the bases of branches near the trunks of trees; the rufous owls roost among foliage. The varied spots of black, white, brown, and pale yellow mixed into their plumage probably developed to imitate the dappled sunlight among the leaves and branches.

Screech owls live in North and South America, while scops owls live in Africa, southern Eurasia, and Southeast Asia. Some of the larger species eat small rodents and songbirds, but many species feed on insects, catching them in flight or by perching and then pouncing.

The word *scops* comes from the Greek word *scopus*, meaning "to see," and was originally used to refer to all owls. Screech owls were named for the eastern screech owl's call.

The calls of most screech owls are extended trills and whinnies, while scops owls' calls are simpler—a series of short notes. Since many of these owls look similar, it is often easier to identify a species by its particular call than by its appearance.

North America's two species of screech owls, the eastern and the western, are related, but they occupy different habitats. The eastern screech owl lives east of the Rocky Mountains in woodlands that feature a mixture of deciduous (plants that shed their leaves) and coniferous trees and shrubs. The western screech owl prefers more open woodlands, riverside forests, and even desert areas with large cacti north and west of the Rockies.

Both species are about the same size, 9 inches (22.9 cm) long, and have similar spotted plumage. The rufous color of the eastern screech owl is fairly common, but it is uncommon in the western species. As with most owls, North American screech owls generally do not migrate, although some northern populations may move south during harsh winters. Others may move from mountain locations to lower-elevation plains.

Eastern and western screech owls prefer to nest close to other members of the same species. Both species nest in holes in trees and even in nesting boxes provided by people. If an animal or even a person comes too close to a nest, the adults may attack by swooping down onto the intruder. Screech owls feed on a wide variety of prey, including insects, reptiles, amphibians, mollusks, rodents, many species of songbirds, and even other screech owls.

This unlucky frog is one of many types of creatures eaten by screech owls. These owls can catch anything from small insects to other screech owls.

Eagle, Fish, and Fishing Owls. This group includes the largest, heaviest owls in the world: the eagle owls. Topped by long ear tufts, their facial disks are not as prominent as in other owl groups, which most likely means that they depend more on sight than hearing for finding food. Their large, golden-yellow to bright orange eyes stand out boldly in their brown facial disks.

The twenty species of eagle owls are widespread, from the Americas to Eurasia, Indonesia, and Africa, although none is found in Australia, New Guinea, and nearby islands.

These highly successful predators occupy a wide variety of habitats, including rain forests, deserts, temperate and boreal forests, or anywhere there are trees or rock outcrops for them to roost and nest on. Their calls range from the classic hoot that most people associate with owls to croaking, hissing, clucking, and even sounds suggesting machines. The call of Fraser's eagle owl is said to sound like a generator.

The Eurasian eagle owl has one of the largest ranges of any eagle owl, including most of Europe and Asia. The birds that live in the north are the largest, reaching 28 inches (71.1 cm) in length and 9 pounds (4.1 kg) in weight. The southern birds are only about 18 inches (45.7 cm) long.

The plumage of these majestic birds is generally dark brown mottled with white above and light brown with black streaks below. The bright white throat is prominently displayed when it inflates while the owl is calling. Eurasian eagle owls are different colors, depending on habitat. Dark colors dominate in the forest dwellers, and lighter colors are more common among birds found in desert habitats.

The eagle owls' powerful talons and sizable bills enable them to hunt large prey such as hares, pheasants, herons, small hawks, foxes, and even small deer. Eagle owls are not picky; they can also live on birds, snakes, small mammals, insects, and even porcupines.

EAGLE OWLS ARE AMONG THE LARGEST OWLS IN THE WORLD. THIS MACKINDER'S EAGLE OWL LIVES IN EASTERN AND SOUTHERN AFRICAOWLS, NESTING ON THE GROUND IN HILLY COUNTRY OR ALONG CLIFFS.

Snowy owls are unlike other owls in that they live in the almost-treeless tundra; they are mostly white in color; and they perch, roost, and nest on the ground. With its eyes closed, this female snowy owl is well camouflaged against the surrounding snow.

This group also includes Asian fish owls and African fishing owls. These two owl subspecies have, like fish eagles and ospreys, developed special adaptations for catching fish. Their feet are unfeathered, and they have spicules—or rough scales on the bottoms of their feet that make it easier to grab and hold on to slippery fish.

Since hearing is less important than sight when hunting fish, the facial disks of both fish owls and fishing owls are even less noticeable than in eagle owls. And since their underwater prey can't hear them approach, they have no need for the soft, noiseless plumage of other owls. After spotting ripples on the water, fish owls and fishing owls swoop down from their perches and snatch their prey from just below the surface with their long, curved talons.

When it comes to size and shape, Asian fish owls differ in important ways from their African cousins. Asian fish owls are as large as eagle owls, and they have large ear tufts. African fishing owls have no ear tufts, but more of a shaggy mane of feathers atop their heads, and they tend to be medium sized, reaching 18 to 24 inches (45.7 to 61 cm).

These owls live near rivers, streams, and lakes. When the waters freeze in winter, fish owls turn to land mammals such as martens (a kind of weasel), hares, and even dogs. Like the eagle owls, the calls of Asian and African fish owls—mostly varied hooting, but also higher-pitched hissing and rattling—are deep and can be heard over long distances.

The snowy owl, with its bright white plumage and tuftless head, blends well into the snow-covered landscape. Like other eagle owls, snowy owls do not have prominent facial disks. Snowy owls are found around the Arctic circle—in far northern Canada and in Greenland, Scandinavia, and Siberia.

Male snowy owls are nearly all white, and females are white with brown spots. Both have thickly feathered feet to insulate them from the cold and to protect them from the potentially sharp bites of their prey, mostly lemmings and other voles. They vary in length from 20 to 24 inches (51 to 61 cm). Males weigh an average of 3.8 pounds (1.7 kg), and the larger females average 4.6 pounds (2.1 kg). Their bright yellow eyes are rimmed by black eyelids and are not as large as some eagle owls' eyes.

Without trees in their habitats, snowy owls nest and perch on the highest ground they can find, which is usually a small hill or exposed rock. This gives them enough of a view to scan the open landscape for small rodents.

Wood and Spectacled Owls. These two groups of medium-sized owls are forest-dwelling species. The twenty-one species of wood owls and four species of spectacled owls have large heads with no ear tufts. Most species are 12 to 23 inches (30.5 to 58.4 cm) long, except for the great gray owl, which is 24 to 27 inches (61 to 68.6 cm) long. Wood and spectacled owls are mostly nocturnal, as their well-developed facial disks indicate. Their large eyes also help them to hunt at pre-dawn or dusk hours, as well as during the day when they have many owlets to feed.

Spectacled owls are found only in South America. Wood owls are found in most of the world, although most species are located in the Americas. Their wide, rounded wings and tails are perfectly suited to maneuvering through the dense forests and jungles where they make their homes.

Like the snowy owl, the great gray owl is widespread in the far north and is the only species of wood owl that lives in both Europe and North America. The large size of this gray and black owl, its relatively small eyes, and its large facial disk distinguish it from all other wood owls.

GREAT GRAY OWLS LIVE IN NORTHERN FORESTS AROUND THE EARTH. THIS SPECIES'
HEARING IS SO ACUTE THAT THEY CAN HUNT RODENTS LIVING UNDER THE WINTER SNOW.

Spectacled owls and wood owls make their nests in holes in trees that are formed by rot and broken limbs or are made by woodpeckers. Some wood owls also use old hawk nests, and the tawny owls of Europe even nest in buildings. Like screech owls, some wood owls are aggressive when defending their nests and may attack intruders.

Songs of wood owls tend to be hoots. Some people remember the call of the barred owl, a wood owl species found in wetland areas of temperate (those regions with a moderate climate) North America, by associating this phrase with it: "Who cooks for you? Who cooks for you all?"

THE DARK MASKS OF SPECTACLED OWLS MAKE THESE BIRDS' PIERCING EYES SEEM EVEN MORE BRILLIANT.

Spectacled owls get their name from the striking masks that are formed by their dark circles of disk feathers surrounded by white plumage around their eyes. The spectacled owl of northern South America has bright yellow eyes that greatly exaggerate the effect. These owls live in dense rain forests, nesting in the holes of large trees. Spectacled owls are called knocking owls in Brazil because of their calls, which sound more like knocks than hoots.

Pygmy Owls. Their diurnal nature and poorly developed facial disks indicate that pygmy owls depend mostly on sight when they hunt. They spend their days on exposed perches, flipping their tails from side to side and scanning the landscape for prey with their piercing yellow eyes. The thirty species of pygmy owls can be found in many countries in the Americas, Africa, Eurasia, and Southeast Asia.

Some pygmy owls have unusual markings on the feathers on the backs of their heads, which form what is called an occipital face. These black markings look like eyes and may prevent larger predators from sneaking up from behind on an unsuspecting pygmy owl. A subgroup called owlets (not to be confused with "baby owls," also called "owlets"), which lives mostly in Africa and Asia, lacks these occipital faces.

Pygmy owls are known for their complicated songs, which involve fluted whistles and trilling notes, often with repeated phrases.

The prey and habitats favored by these small owls vary greatly by species. The 6-inch-long (15.2-cm-long) Andean pygmy owl lives and nests in open woodlands of the Andes Mountains in South America, feeding on small birds, mammals, and insects. The pearl-spotted owlet prefers open savannas—grasslands with scattered shrubs and small trees—in central and southern Africa. Its large talons allow it to catch larger insects and bats, snatching them from the air.

Eurasian pygmy owls prefer to live in northern coniferous forests with large trees and clearings in which they hunt the abundant rodents—voles, shrews, and mice—found in the region. As with most pygmy owls, these owls are very small, about 2 to 2.5 ounces (56.7 to 70.9 g) in weight and 6 to 7 inches (15.2 to 17.8 cm) in length.

As their name indicates, pygmy owls are among the smallest owls in the world. Most species hunt at dawn and dusk.

Elf Owl. In the arid desert regions of central Mexico and the southwestern United States, elf owls can be seen poking their heads out of their nest holes in the tall, treelike saguaro cacti. They are strictly nocturnal, probably in order to avoid the daytime desert heat, and they hunt mostly insects.

These are the smallest owls in the world, measuring only 5 to 5.5 inches (12.7 to 14 cm) in length and weighing only 1.25 to 1.5 ounces (35.4 to 42.5 g). Their songs are made up of a series of loud whistled or yelping phrases. Unusual among owls, the males are said to share in the incubation of the eggs and take turns with the females sitting on the nest.

Little Owls. Two of the four species of these small owls are mostly diurnal. Burrowing owls of North America spend much of their time perched on the ground or on fence posts in prairies, pastures, and farmlands in western North America, central Mexico, and eastern South America from Brazil to Patagonia. Like many small owls, they feed mainly on insects, but occasionally eat small mammals and reptiles.

These unusually long-legged owls make their nests in the ground in old prairie dog burrows, or they may dig a burrow of their own up to 3.25 feet (1 meter) deep with a winding tunnel. One of only two owl species known to bring material to the nest, burrowing owls line the entrance with cattle dung to discourage predators.

LITTLE OWLS ARE WIDESPREAD THROUGHOUT EUROPE, ASIA, AND NORTH AFRICA. THEY HUNT MAINLY INSECTS AND ARE FREQUENTLY FOUND AROUND FARMS, HELPING FARMERS BY EATING PESTS THAT DAMAGE CROPS.

Little owls—the species for which this group is named—are found throughout Eurasia and North Africa. Like burrowing owls, little owls also favor open areas such as farms and grasslands. They have chunky bodies with short tails and flat heads. Like others of this group, their facial disks do not stand out. They are about 8 to 9 inches (20.3 to 22.9 cm) long and weigh about 3.5 to 6 ounces (99.2 to 170.1 g).

Forest Owls. Three of the four species in this group live only in the Americas, while the boreal owl has a wide distribution across northern North America and Eurasia. The boreal owl, also known as Tengmalm's owl in Europe, prefers moss-covered trees in northern coniferous forests. They use woodpecker holes in large old trees for their nests. Boreal owls have rectangular heads with no ear tufts. Their large facial disks enable them to hear their prey—small rodents—in their dark, tree-filled habitats.

Boreal owls often become prey for the larger tawny owls. This and the destruction of forests have made these once-widespread owls much less common now than in the past.

The northern saw-whet owl, named for its rasping song, which some say sounds like a saw being sharpened, is found in the moist woodlands of North America. These owls have huge eyes set in a round head that seems large for their very small bodies—they measure only 7 inches (17.8 cm) in length.

Hawk Owls. Of the twenty-three species that make up this group of owls, all but two—the Madagascar hawk owl and the northern hawk owl—live in Southeast Asia and Australasia.

As their name suggests, hawk owls are the most hawklike of all owls, with long, pointed wings and long tails. None of the hawk owls has ear tufts. Some species have rounded heads, while other, larger species have eyebrow ridges, similar to hawks. Small ear openings and the lack of pronounced facial

THE NORTHERN SAW-WHET OWL OFTEN PERCHES IN SHRUBS AND LOW BRANCHES, AS IN THIS ROSEBUSH IN BRITISH COLUMBIA.

disks mean that hawk owls hunt mostly by sight, although they are generally nocturnal.

Hawk owls range in size from the Philippine hawk owl, 6 to 8 inches (15 to 20 cm) long, to the largest owl in Australia, the appropriately named powerful owl, 21.5 to 24.5 inches (55 to 63 cm) long. The powerful owl has long legs with strong feet that can clutch large mammals, such as opossums. The varied calls of powerful owls include hoots, barks, whistles, and croaks.

Northern hawk owls' unusually bold black-and-white plumage, along with their bright yellow eyes set in a white facial disk rimmed with black, give these owls a sharp, intense appearance. Like many boreal raptors, northern hawk owls feed mostly on small rodents, such as voles.

Eared Owls. True to their name, the seven species of eared owls have prominent ear tufts. They also have long wings, short tails, and well-defined facial disks, which help them in their role as efficient nocturnal hunters.

The eared owls can be divided into two groups: the long-eared owls and the short-eared owls. Long-eared, Stygian, Abyssinian long-eared, Madagascar long-eared, and striped owls are the five species of long-eared owls, while short-eared and marsh owls are the two species of short-eared owls. The owls in the short-eared group have smaller ear tufts near the tops of their heads, while the long-eared owls' tufts are longer and sit on the middle of their heads.

These two groups differ in their choice of habitat as well. The long-eared owl species are open woodland species, living mostly in temperate and tropical areas of the Americas and Africa. Both short-eared owl species prefer open habitats near wetlands or swampy areas with scattered trees in colder temperate zones. Only the long-eared owls and the short-eared owl species themselves are migratory; the other eared owls are yearlong residents of their habitats.

Long-eared owls can be heard at dusk as their calls ring out in forests, advertising their presence to their young and mates. This species has a wide distribution, ranging from Canada and the United States to much of Eurasia and the northern edge of Africa. They hunt low along forest edges, flushing small rodents, which they pounce on suddenly.

Because they prefer open habitats, short-eared owls make their nests in shallow holes near clumps of grass or other vegetation in wet meadows or marshes. Despite their wide distribution across much of the Northern Hemisphere and southern South America, their preference for open habitats leaves them vulnerable to pesticides and habitat destruction. As a result, their numbers have declined in some areas.

IN FLIGHT, THE LONG-EARED OWL'S EAR TUFTS ARE NEARLY INVISIBLE. WHEN THE OWL HAS PERCHED AND IS ATTEMPTING TO BLEND IN, ITS EAR TUFTS ARE ERECT.

Short-eared owls perform elaborate courtship displays involving aerial acrobatics, dives, and wing clapping—quickly bringing their wings together in flight. Short-eared owls can be active during the day, but they are most often active at dusk and at night.

4 Owls in Detail

As nighttime predators, owls have evolved physical adaptations and skills that no other group of birds possesses. Exceptional powers of hearing and sight, in addition to their ability to silently and swiftly pounce on their prey, make them among the most unusual and effective predators on the planet.

Size and Shape

The general appearance of owls is unlike that of most other birds—even hawks, their ecological counterparts, and nightjars, their closest living relatives.

An owl's skull is shaped to accommodate its large eyes, ears, and relatively large brain. These are an owl's most important tools, next to its talons and beak.

Like hawks, owls have an extremely strong yet lightweight skeleton. Some of the bones are hollow, but they have struts within those bones that give them support without adding excess weight. For example, a great horned owl's skeleton

BARN OWLS SWOOP SOUNDLESSLY DOWN UPON THEIR PREY, GUIDED BY THEIR EXCEPTIONAL HEARING AND POWERFUL EYESIGHT.

makes up only 8.6 percent of the bird's total body weight, while an adult human's skeleton makes up about twenty percent of the total body weight.

An owl's largest muscles are the ones used for flight. They are firmly anchored to their strong keel bones, which protect the rib cage from being crushed by the powerful force exerted when owls flap their wings.

In general, female owls are about 25 percent larger than male owls. A similar size difference can be seen in most hawks. Scientists are uncertain about the reasons for this difference, but they think it has something to do with competition for prey. The larger females and smaller males can concentrate on catching larger or smaller prey, respectively, when feeding their endlessly hungry young. That way they increase the number of potential food sources, thus being more assured of finding meals.

Sight

One characteristic that owls do not share with any other birds is that their eyes face *forward*, not to the sides. Even the eyes of their fellow predators, hawks, are on the sides of their heads. Other birds have wider fields of vision. Woodcocks can see 360 degrees, all the way around their heads, because their eyes are located so far to the sides. But their binocular vision, in which each eye's field of vision overlaps with the other's to show depth, is poor.

Owls, on the other hand, have a field of vision of only 110 degrees, but their binocular vision is greater than that of any other bird—about 50 to 70 percent of their total vision. This means that they can gauge spacing among and distance between objects better, which is helpful when finding and chasing other birds that are flying through the forest or mammals

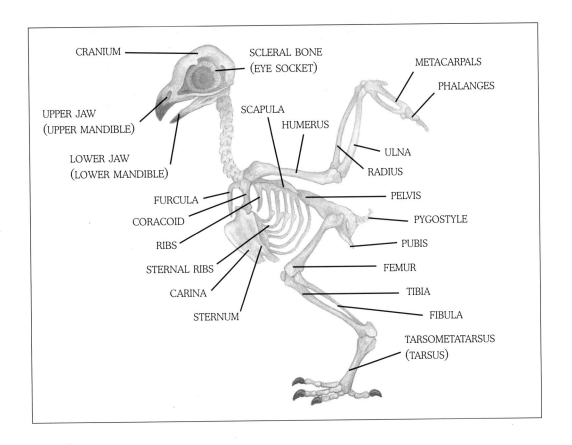

CRANIUM

SCLERAL BONE
(EYE SOCKET)

METACARPALS

PHALANGES

UPPER JAW
(UPPER MANDIBLE)

SCAPULA

HUMERUS

ULNA

RADIUS

LOWER JAW
(LOWER MANDIBLE)

FURCULA

CORACOID

RIBS

STERNAL RIBS

CARINA

STERNUM

PELVIS

PYGOSTYLE

PUBIS

FEMUR

TIBIA

FIBULA

TARSOMETATARSUS
(TARSUS)

OWLS' SKELETONS ARE VERY LIGHTWEIGHT BUT VERY STRONG.

that are moving along the ground amid stumps and plants in dim light.

Rings of fixed bones hold their eyes in place in the sockets, so owls cannot move their eyes independently of their heads. To compensate for this, owls have extremely flexible necks (they have twice the number of vertebrae as humans). They can swivel their heads 270 degrees around and look directly over their backs to keep track of moving targets.

Owls are able to see better at night than any other bird, but they can also see equally well during the day. An owl's visual

Although hearing is the major tool that many owl species use for detecting prey, owls may have the sharpest vision of any animals, both in their ability to see in dim light and in their spatial perception.

sensitivity may be from thirty-five to one hundred times greater than a human's.

While most creatures are able to either see fine details or see well in the dark, owls are able to do both. Most animals' eyes are round or oval shaped. Owls have tubular-shaped eyes, which enables them to see distant objects very well.

Their eyelids are unusual in the bird world as well. Owls blink with their upper eyelids, like humans and other primates, and they sleep with their lower eyelids closed. Like hawks, owls also have a third, translucent eyelid called the nictitating membrane. It closes to protect the eye from strong light and physical damage, allowing the birds to see as they fly through dense brush after prey.

Hearing

Even though owls have exceptionally large, strong eyes, they still need acute hearing to be able to detect prey at night. Owls' ears are most sensitive to high-pitched noises such as squeaking and rustling—the sounds that usually mean food is near.

The size of an owl's ears depends on the size and species of the owl. Their ears are merely openings in the sides of their heads, hidden and protected by feathers. These openings extend from near the top of the skull to either side of the lower jaw. Barn owls have rounded ear openings, while the ears of true owls are much more varied.

The many tiny feathers on an owl's face make up the very special tool called a facial disk. It amplifies and focuses sound toward their ears. These disks, as well as the ears themselves, are larger and better developed in species that are more active at night, such as long-eared, barn, gray, and tawny owls. These species rely more on sound than sight to locate their prey.

Species with less developed facial disks, such as hawk owls, are usually less nocturnal—they are more active during the day or at dawn and dusk.

One of the reasons that owls are so good at locating their prey in the dark is that the ear openings in their heads are not symmetrical. One ear, usually the right, is lower than the other.

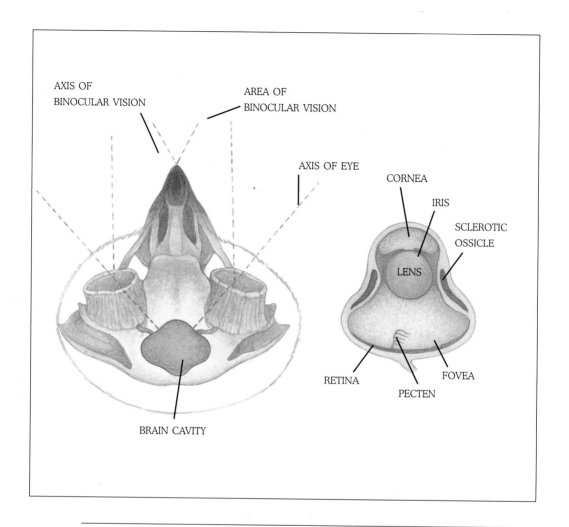

AXIS OF
BINOCULAR VISION

AREA OF
BINOCULAR VISION

AXIS OF EYE

CORNEA

IRIS

SCLEROTIC
OSSICLE

LENS

RETINA

PECTEN

FOVEA

BRAIN CAVITY

OWLS' EYES TAKE UP A HUGE PART OF THEIR HEADS AND ARE ANCHORED IN PLACE,
FORCING THE BIRDS TO MOVE THEIR HEADS IN ORDER TO LOOK AROUND.

Detecting the difference in the amount of time it takes for sounds to reach each ear provides owls with another dimension of sound. Lowering their heads so the sound is equally loud in both ears, owls can determine the precise location of a mouse's scratching and squeaking in the dark or a bird's location among the dense leaves of a tree.

Feathers

Birds have five distinct feather types that make up their plumage:

1. The main feathers that cover a bird's body are known as contour feathers and include the wing feathers, called remiges, and the tail feathers, called retrices.
2. The soft, fluffy feathers known as down feathers lie close to a bird's skin, trapping body heat and keeping the bird warm.
3. Semiplumes serve as filler between the contour and down feathers.

OWL EARS ARE SIMPLY OPENINGS IN THE SIDES OF THEIR HEADS AND ARE HIDDEN BY FEATHERS. THE EARS OF BARN OWL SPECIES, LIKE THE OWL PICTURED ABOVE, ARE ROUND IN SHAPE, WHILE THE EARS OF TRUE OWLS HAVE MORE VARIED SHAPES.

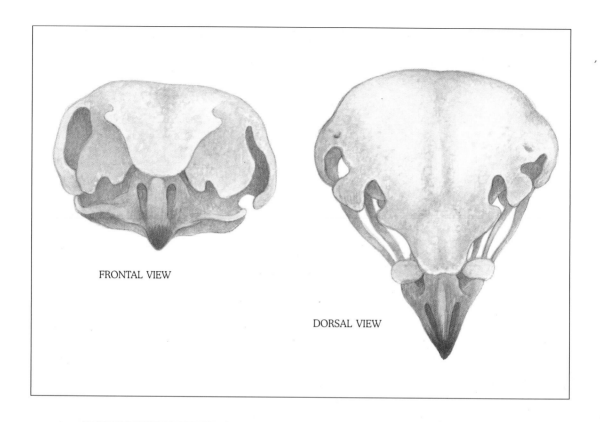

FRONTAL VIEW

DORSAL VIEW

THE SKULL OF A BOREAL OWL SHOWS HOW ASYMMETRICAL THE EAR OPENINGS ARE. THIS HELPS THE OWLS TO PINPOINT THE EXACT LOCATION OF THEIR PREY.

4.   Filoplumes are thin, wispy feathers that are sensitive to the movement of the other feathers as they respond to wind or rain, for example. These can tell a bird that its flight feathers are out of alignment and need to be adjusted.

5.   The small, stiff feathers around the eyes and the base of the beak are known as bristles.

The colors of owls' plumage are various shades of brown, black, gray, and white. Rather than making them stand out as some birds' feather coats do, these colors actually help an owl

THE COLOR AND PATTERN OF MOST OWLS' FEATHER COATS CLOSELY MATCH THEIR ENVIRONMENTS. THE PLUMAGE OF FOREST SPECIES VISUALLY BLENDS WITH THE BARK OF THE TREES IN WHICH THEY ROOST.

not to be seen by matching the bird's environment. The great gray owl's gray feathers blend in with the northern forest's gray-barked coniferous trees. The plumage of forest owls is spotted, a pattern matching the broken sunlight as it filters through the trees onto leaves, branches, and bark. The white plumage of the snowy owl is suited perfectly to its snowy habitat, the tundra.

An owl usually rests during the day on a tree branch close to the trunk. If disturbed, it will straighten its body, raise its ear tufts (if it has them), and close its eyes. By doing this an owl can blend even more seamlessly into the color and pattern of the tree bark.

While the males and females of most bird species have distinct differences in plumage colors, owls do not. But some owl species come in more than one color, like screech owls. The mostly gray western screech owls blend in with the bark of trees found in coniferous forests of the north and west. Eastern screech owls are usually rufous, a color that makes it easier to hide against the reddish-brown bark of many deciduous trees in the eastern United States.

Owls must take good care of their feathers if they want to keep them sleek and healthy. When at rest, owls preen their feathers, running them through their beaks and straightening out the barbs. Owls also coat their feathers by taking oil from a gland at the base of their tails with their beaks and rubbing it on their feathers as they preen. The barn owls are different from the true owls in that they have a comblike edge on their inner talons that they use when preening the feathers on their heads.

In a process called molting, owls also grow a whole new set of feathers every year. They lose their old, worn flight feathers in an orderly process, from the inside of their wings to the outside. They also lose them symmetrically, one at a time on each wing. The whole process takes about three months to complete. If it happened any quicker, the owl might not be able to fly, would be in danger from predators, and could be unable to catch its food.

Mobbing. An owl's plumage is effective camouflage, increasing its chances of not being detected by predators during the day as it rests on its roost. But it can also be effective against a danger of another sort.

Many species of songbird rightfully see hawks and owls as threats, since many of these predators hunt small birds. If a songbird foraging for seeds or insects discovers a roosting owl, it will raise the alarm, alerting nearby birds with a special call. Other birds of the same species or even different species will flock to the tree, calling and flying around the owl. This is called mobbing.

This is the songbird's way of telling the owl they have seen it, and it is also an attempt to drive the owl out of the area. If the owl is discovered, it often has no choice but to find another roost, using some precious energy to do so.

Flight

With all these amazing tools, it is hard to imagine an owl needing anything else. These special adaptations would be less effective, however, if the owl's prey could hear the bird approaching. Fortunately for owls, they are silent fliers. Any excessive sound would not only alert the prey to the owl's presence, but it might also interfere with the owl's hearing, the sense it relies on most to find its food.

When most birds' wings flap, they make noise as the air moves through them. On owls, the leading edges of the primary flight feathers are delicately fringed and softly textured, features that break up the movement of air through their wings, dampening the sound. As a result, most owls are silent as they fly. Owls that hunt during the day and at dusk and those that search out fish rely less on hearing, so their wing feathers do not have these adaptations. Their wings make noise like other birds'.

Different owl species have different wing shapes depending upon the habitat they hunt in. Forest owls' wings are short and rounded, which helps the birds maneuver better when flying

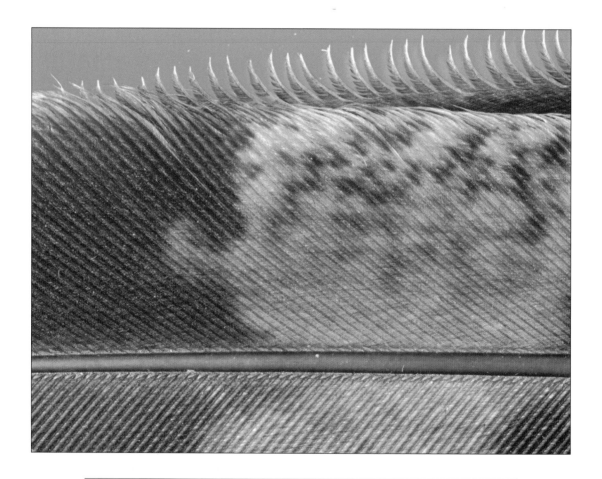

THE SOFT TEXTURE AND FRINGES ON THE EDGES OF AN OWL'S FLIGHT FEATHERS REDISTRIBUTE THE MOVEMENT OF AIR THROUGH ITS WINGS, MAKING THEM SILENT FLIERS.

among closely spaced trees. Owls that migrate, such as long-eared and short-eared owls, have longer and more pointed wings, which allow the birds to fly long distances.

However, most owls have a large wing surface compared to their body size. This allows them to fly with little effort, almost floating on air. When they are not flapping their wings, owls keep them cupped or bowed downward.

Beak and Talons

Once an owl finds its chosen prey using its ears and eyes and quickly flies to it on silent wings, the predator needs powerful, efficient tools for grabbing and killing it. This is where the talons and beak come in.

The great force that an owl uses when pouncing on its prey is intended to kill or cripple the animal swiftly. There is a lot of power behind that pounce, so the feet have to be very strong to withstand the impact. An owl's feet are large and sturdy in those species, such as eagle owls, that hunt large prey, and less so in smaller owls that hunt insects.

All birds have four toes, three that point forward and one that points toward the back. Owls have the special ability to swivel their front outer toe to the back when carrying prey or perching. This gives them a much stronger grip. Rough ridges or scales on the bottoms of their feet also help them to grasp prey even more firmly.

The toes end in razor-sharp talons that can instantly pierce the hide of any creature, puncturing its vital organs. Talons are made of a bonelike substance called keratin. The size and color of talons depend on the species of owl, but they vary from black to ivory.

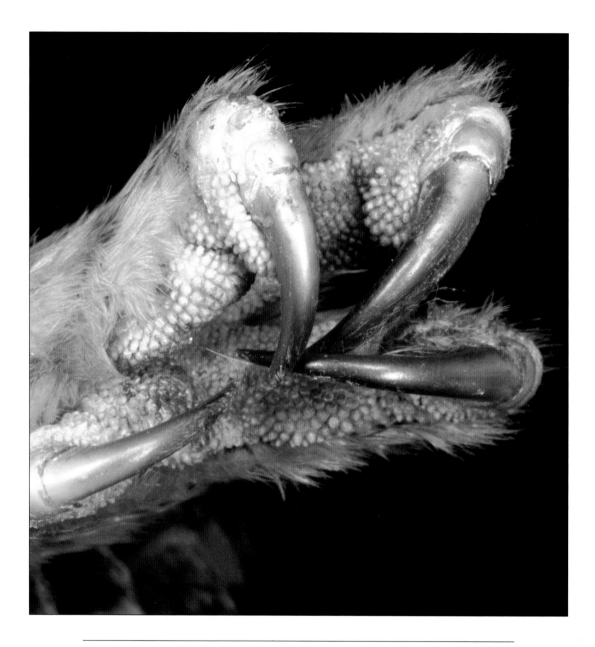

THE POWERFUL FEET AND SHARP TALONS OF OWLS ARE EFFECTIVE TOOLS FOR CAP-
TURING AND QUICKLY IMMOBILIZING THEIR PREY.

Once the prey has been caught and crippled by the powerful talons, an owl uses its strong beak to crush its victim's head. This ensures that the animal is dead and helps it go down easier when swallowed. The edges of an owl's beak are very sharp. They can easily slice up larger prey into smaller, bite-sized pieces.

An owl's beak has also evolved to help the bird see better. The beak points downward, thus intruding less on the bird's field of vision. The small nostrils at the base of an owl's beak are an indication that smell is of little importance to these hunters.

5 Behavior

Although owls have evolved amazing, unique physical adaptations, the way they use these features is what makes these birds remarkable nighttime predators. Such effectiveness has helped them to settle in almost every available habitat on Earth, from tundra to desert to rain forest.

Habitats and Territories

Except for the breeding season, owls are mostly solitary creatures. They spend their nights hunting and their days roosting in trees or caves or on the ground, where they can sleep, digest, and preen in peace. Some owls—such as barn, long-eared, and short-eared owls—do occasionally roost in groups of their own species.

Some species of owls are faithful to specific roosting spots, using a location for a long time, until some major change or disturbance occurs, such as the roosting tree getting blown down in a storm or a new, more powerful predator moving into their territory. Other owls, such as the tawny owl, constantly change the location of their roosts.

THE GREAT HORNED OWL HOLDS ITS PREY, A HOUSE MOUSE, IN ITS MOUTH.

The larger area where an owl chooses to make its home is known as its home range. An owl's hunting territory within this range is determined by the type of prey it hunts. If the prey is abundant and concentrated in a small area, the owl will usually have a small hunting range. Owls that hunt insects, such as pygmy owls, have small hunting ranges. Larger owls that hunt more widespread prey, such as eagle owls, will have larger hunting ranges.

During breeding season, when owls are raising their young, the birds have a nesting territory in addition to their hunting range. Some species, such as snowy owls, do not hunt within

BURROWING OWLS NEST IN PRAIRIE DOG BURROWS OR, IN THIS CASE, A TERMITE MOUND IN BRAZIL.

their nesting territory. Responding to this, snow geese actually make their own nests near the snowy owls' nests. Within the owls' nesting territories, the geese are safe from the snowy owls and many other predators, which the owls chase away in order to protect their own nests and young.

Some owl species migrate seasonally between two home ranges. Their breeding range ideally has several suitable nesting sites and is near an area with plentiful prey. When the breeding season is over, usually at the onset of winter or the dry season, when prey is less available, the owls disperse to their winter or nonbreeding range. They may travel great distances to a warmer or wetter location where food is more abundant. From Europe and Asia, birds often travel into tropical and subtropical Africa, and birds breeding in North America move into Central and South America for the winter.

Common scops owls migrate between summer breeding ranges in southern Europe and parts of central Asia and winter ranges in the savannas of West and East Africa. Some birds travel from 4,350 to 5,000 miles (7,000 to 8,050 km) between Siberia and Ethiopia.

However, many owl species stay put, moving at most from mountainous areas to lowlands for the winter. Owls seem to be able to deal with seasonal changes better than other birds. Some owls hunt well even in the snow.

Migratory owls defend only their breeding territories, but year-round residents often permanently occupy and defend one territory. When an intruder approaches too close to the nest site, owls may attack aggressively, swooping down and pouncing on it.

EACH OWL SPECIES HAS A DISTINCTIVE CALL, WHICH IT USES TO ESTABLISH ITS TERRITORY AND IDENTIFY OTHERS OF ITS OWN KIND.

Since owls that nest on the ground are more exposed, they will stand firm against predators such as foxes, which often prey on both young birds and eggs. Snowy owls will fluff out their feathers, spread their tails and wings, and hiss or clack their beaks. This makes them appear larger and more threatening. They may even rock their heads or bodies from side to side.

If this doesn't scare the fox away, the owl parents will try to distract it and draw it away from the nest by pretending to be injured. They may drag a wing along the ground as if it were broken. Once they've lured the fox away, the owl will spring up into the air, scaring the fox, or dive at it.

Owls advertise their ownership of a particular territory. Diurnal owls do this with a showy display, flying around the site and clapping their wings. Since a visual display would not be very useful in the dark, nocturnal owls make their presence known by using their voices.

Vocalizations

Owls have a variety of different calls, even within the same species. These vocalizations are part of a rich and complex language that distinguishes owls from other birds and from one another. These calls range from the well-known hoots to barks, squeals, buzzes, coughs, and even screams. Some owl calls could be mistaken for insect or frog sounds. The voice of the barking owl, a species of hawk owl from Australia and New Guinea, has been likened to a dog's bark or even a woman's scream.

The names of some owls are taken from the sounds of their calls. The morepork, a small New Zealand hawk owl, and the boobook, from Australia, have similar calls that sound like their names. The calls are written out by ornithologists as *quor-quo* or *cu-coo*. *Bubo*, the scientific name for the genus of eagle owls, is

taken from the sound of the Eurasian eagle owl's call, sometimes written as *búho*.

Establishing territory is one of the main reasons that owls call or vocalize. When a barred owl hoots, others in the forest that can hear its sounds will answer. These calls help communicate where territories are, giving the owls a mental image of their surroundings. Each owl can also identify other individual owls by the peculiar characteristics of their calls. A weak call will indicate to the others that the owl is sick or injured. A male owl without a territory of its own will quickly move in to take it over by chasing the sick one out.

Hooting occurs most frequently in spring and autumn, but especially at the beginning of the breeding season when the males are trying to attract potential mates. For mating pairs that had already been established in a previous breeding season, the male's hooting will stimulate the female to prepare for mating.

Hooting to attract a possible mate is done from an open, exposed location—on a high perch like a tree branch or a rocky outcrop—because, for some species, it is important for the female to see as well as hear the male. The male owl's posture, the swelling of its throat as the owl inflates it to call, and the call itself are all signs of the male's fitness to breed. The female will choose the strongest, healthiest male available.

The larger the owl, the deeper the song and usually, the larger the territory. Small pygmy owls have high-pitched voices and relatively small ranges. Large eagle owls have deep bass hoots and hunt over broad areas. Low-pitched calls carry farther than high-pitched ones in open areas. Snowy owls have very deep calls. Their calls can carry great distances over the open, treeless terrain, which is necessary for a species with such a large territory.

Hoots are not the only sounds owls make. They have a variety of different calls for various functions. The young have specific begging calls to tell their parents they are hungry. There are also calls to warn of danger, to tell others that an owl is angry, and softer calls that males use to invite females to the nest. When they feel threatened, owls will sometimes make a clucking sound with their beaks as a warning to potential intruders.

Hunting

Owls hunt a wide variety of creatures, and these highly skilled birds of prey need to eat a lot to support their high metabolism.

Larger owls hunt larger, more diverse prey. They are less picky about what they hunt and spend more time hunting because their quarry usually has a more extensive range as well. Smaller owls spend less time hunting, choosing smaller, more plentiful prey that is concentrated in one area.

The method an owl uses for hunting depends on both the owl and its victim. Most owls hunt from a perch where they have had success before, watching and waiting quietly for the telltale sounds of their prey. The owls bob their heads up and down, listening, to get a precise fix on their quarry before flying off the perch in pursuit.

Barn owls have two ways of hunting. In the dark, they flap their wings as they fly toward the prey, swinging their feet. When they are positioned directly over the mouse or other creature, they pull their wings back, thrust their feet forward, and seize the animal. If they are hunting at dusk or even in daylight, they do not flap their wings but glide to their prey, keeping their feet tucked behind them. When they are above the animal, they will grab it just as they do in the dark. Barn owls can find their quarry in total darkness.

Great gray owls of the boreal forests also hunt from a perch, but in winter they sometimes have to rely entirely on their hearing, even in daylight. They listen for sounds of voles, shrews, or mice moving in their tunnels and burrows beneath the snow. Once a great gray owl has located a likely meal, it flies toward it over the snow, hovers above it to make sure it has found the exact spot, then plunges down headfirst into the deep snow. The owl then pulls its feet forward to grab its prey. Great gray owls

SMALLER OWLS LIKE THIS LITTLE OWL ARE VERY QUICK AND THEY MANEUVER EASILY, ENABLING THEM TO CATCH INSECTS IN THE AIR.

have been known to grab rodents as far down as 18 inches (45.7 cm) into the snow.

Insectivorous owls, such as pygmy and scops owls, can move swiftly and deftly, able to snatch insects or bats out of the air as well as from the ground or in foliage. Fish and fishing owls either hunt from a perch, watching for fish to come near the surface, or they wait on the banks of a stream for their prey, sometimes even wading into shallow water.

An owl's prey is usually so stunned by the impact of the bird's descent that it is paralyzed. The owl then uses its strong beak to crush the creature's head. If the food is small enough, like a mouse or a shrew, the owl will swallow it whole on the spot. Larger prey is carried away to a safe location and torn to pieces before swallowing. Whole prey is also brought back to the nest and picked apart for the young.

Pellets and Digestion

Owls can digest soft material such as meat and muscle fairly easily. The food an owl eats passes into the glandular stomach, where it is softened by enzymes and acids. The material then moves into the gizzard, the second part of the owl's stomach. Strong muscles in the gizzard grind the soft parts and pass them on to the small intestine, from which the food becomes absorbed into the body.

But bones, hair, and feathers are not as easy to digest. These are collected in the gizzard, where they form a plug the size and shape of the gizzard. This plug, or pellet, as it is called, travels back up into the glandular stomach. After about ten hours, the owl regurgitates, or vomits, the pellet out. A pellet usually contains the indigestible parts of a few meals eaten over several hours' time. After a pellet is formed, an owl cannot eat again until the pellet is regurgitated.

Owls usually leave piles of pellets at their favorite roosts. Researchers have been able to discover a lot about different owls' diets by collecting and examining these pellets. They are often full of the unbroken bones of the owls' smaller prey. These bones and fur or feathers can be identified, and collectively they offer a picture of what the owls have been eating.

Pellets are also a good way for scientists to keep track of the numbers and species of rodents in a given area. These small, secretive creatures can be hard to detect, so pellet analysis is often the first clue of the presence of a particular species.

OWL PELLETS ARE AS DISTINCTIVE AS THEIR CALLS. THE SIZE, SHAPE, AND CONTENTS OF THE PELLET CAN PROVIDE IMPORTANT CLUES TO THE SPECIES OF OWL THAT COUGHED IT UP.

Changes in a habitat, such as when a meadow is converted into a pasture, can prompt a change in which small mammal species live there. The pellets of owls will show this change.

Pellet analysis has also allowed researchers to clear the name of the little owl in Great Britain. In the early twentieth century, these owls were widely thought by the public to be responsible for taking livestock and game birds, despite the fact that Italian gardeners encouraged little owls near their plots to get rid of insects.

When the British Trust for Ornithology undertook a study of pellets in 1935, the researchers discovered numerous exoskeletons but very few bones in the pellets of these owls. It was clear that the little owls' main prey was a variety of insects, many of

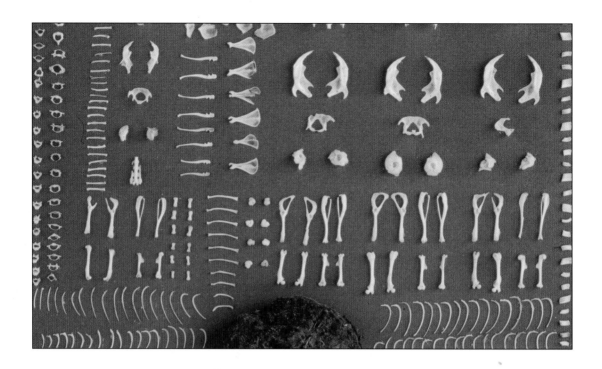

THESE BONES—FROM THREE FIELD VOLES AND ONE HARVEST MOUSE—WERE FOUND IN A SINGLE BARN OWL PELLET IN ENGLAND.

which are known pests to farmers and gardeners. This made people realize that the owls were a beneficial presence and should not be killed.

Spotting Owls in the Wild. Owling, or the practice of finding and watching owls, can be a difficult but rewarding activity. Since owls are active mostly at night and stick to their roosts by day, they are hard for people to spot and observe. Even experienced birders usually don't have many owls on their life lists—lists of all the birds they have ever seen.

Birding at night seems like an odd thing to do; the usual visual clues are not helpful in identifying a species. Since owls' calls are very distinctive, it's often easier to identify each species by its call. Getting familiar with the calls of the owl species living within a particular area is a good start in figuring out "who" is around.

There are some characteristic differences between owls and hawks that will make daytime identification easier: The major clue is the general shape of the bird. Hawks have smaller, more distinct heads; owls' large heads appear to blend into their bodies and make them seem almost headless. Many owls also have ear tufts, while hawks do not. A few hawk species have crests, but these look nothing like owls' ear tufts.

Another important difference between owls and hawks is the way they fly. Owls fly with their wings cupped, or bowed downward, in between flaps. When gliding, hawks fly with their wings straight out or slightly raised. Another clue is whether or not the bird makes any noise when flying. If not, then it is most likely an owl.

An excellent clue as to whether owls are in a particular area is the presence of pellets on the ground. There may be piles of them found at the base of a favorite roost tree. Experts can even tell which species of owl created a certain pellet by looking at its shape, color, and contents. Pellets are not harmful or toxic and can be handled safely. They can be broken apart, revealing bones and even whole skulls of the creatures eaten.

People often get frustrated by their lack of success in trying to spot owls, but even the best birders don't see an owl every time they go out. Seeing an owl one out of ten tries is a good average. Talking to local bird and owl experts is an excellent way to learn more.

6 Breeding

M uch of an owl pair's time is devoted to the long and complex process of raising their young. Everything from selecting good hunting territories, preening, and remaining healthy and strong to finding safe roosts and avoiding predators will eventually determine whether or not individual owls are able to attract mates and reproduce.

Owls start the breeding season earlier and take longer to raise their young than most birds. And some species, such as barn owls, may raise more than one brood a year.

Breeding territories have to provide the owls with suitable nesting sites and a plentiful source of food, because young owls grow quickly and, like their parents, have active metabolisms.

Choosing a Nest

When warm weather begins in the temperate or boreal zone, or when the rains start in the tropics, male owls begin their yearly chore of searching out and inspecting nesting sites. Male owls of

THIS GREAT HORNED OWL DID NOT MAKE THIS NEST BUT PROBABLY TOOK IT OVER FROM A RAVEN OR OTHER LARGE BIRD.

migratory species return to the breeding territories before the females each year to perform this advance scouting.

Unlike most other birds, owls do not make their own nests. In many cases, they let other birds do the work for them. In this regard, they are similar to some falcon species, which nest on cliffs and rooftops or use old crow or hawk nests.

The vast majority of owls prefer to nest in holes in trees. This means that their breeding habitat must include mature trees that have holes large enough for the owls to make their nests in. These holes are created by rot, broken branches, or woodpeckers, which excavate holes for their own nests.

The only owls that generally do not nest in natural tree hollows are eagle owls, grass owls, eared owls, and burrowing owls. But owls are adaptable, and species that normally nest in tree holes may nest on the ground if there are no holes available.

Wood and eagle owls often use the abandoned nests of hawks or eagles. Most owls are early nesters, so they are able to claim a nest or territory before other species of raptors arrive to breed. If they can, owls will use the same nests for many years. The owls do not maintain these nests, so they gradually fall apart and become unusable. This is why owls usually have more than one nesting site in their territories.

Owls that live in open habitats, such as tundra and grasslands, tend to be ground- or cliff-nesters. Snowy owls scratch out a shallow hole on high ground. Eagle owls will use a rock ledge or cliff as a nesting site.

When living in a wooded setting, barn owls will nest in hollow trees. Many of these owls have also become adapted to human settlement, and—true to their names—they will nest in human-made structures, including barns, churches, and other buildings.

SNOWY OWLS NEST ON HIGH GROUND OR ON BOULDERS IN THE TREELESS TUNDRA.
THIS PROVIDES THEM A GOOD VANTAGE POINT FOR SCANNING FOR BOTH PREDATORS
AND PREY.

Romance

Male owls hoot to signal the beginning of the breeding season. These calls are attempts to attract females to their territory and to ward off other males. An interested female owl approaching an unmated male's territory needs to give the right response in order to be allowed to enter. The voices of female owls are usually higher pitched than, and thus distinguishable from, the males' voices.

A male owl will fly from nesting site to nesting site under the watchful gaze of its chosen or potential mate, stopping to sing at

MATED OWLS OFTEN ASSIST EACH OTHER WITH PREENING, ESPECIALLY WITH THE FEATHERS ON THE BACK OF THE HEAD AND NECK.

each site. The male may also offer food to the female to entice her. Only after the female has chosen the final nesting site will the pair begin mating.

Courtship displays may involve aerial acrobatics, with male owls showing off their flying ability. They may circle around the nesting site, as with snowy owls, or they may clap their wings, as with short-eared owls.

Owls prepare for mating by rocking back and forth, fluffing their feathers, opening their beaks wide, rubbing cheeks with each other, and clicking their beaks. The female murmurs a series of soft calls, inviting the male to mount. The male balances on her back, steadying himself with his wings and holding on to her neck with his beak.

Most owl pairs are monogamous, meaning they mate for life. Once mated pairs are established, the owls often roost together. Males and females also clean and straighten each other's plumage, paying particular attention to the normally hard-to-reach feathers on the face and the back of the head and neck.

Incubation

Owl eggs are white and fairly round, like balls. The tapered oval shape of other birds' eggs prevents them from rolling easily out of their nests. Since most owls nest in holes in trees, the eggs don't need to be oval, because there is little danger of them falling out and breaking.

Some hawks and falcons lay a fixed number of eggs, regardless of habitat conditions. The amount of food available to an owl pair determines the number of eggs the female lays. Large owls such as the Eurasian eagle owl may lay only one egg, while smaller owls such as the burrowing owl may lay up to twelve but usually produce around five. If there is an abundance of food

SNOWY OWLS ARE THOUGHT TO HAVE A WEAKER PAIR BOND THAN MOST OWL
SPECIES, WHICH OFTEN MATE FOR LIFE.

available, as when lemming populations peak in the far north, a
snowy owl will lay up to twelve eggs, more than its usual clutch
(a group of eggs laid by one female) of seven to nine. When
lemmings are scarce, snowy owls may not breed at all.

Female owls lay their individual eggs about two days apart.
When they lay large clutches, that means there may be as many
as two weeks between the laying of the first egg and the last.
The eggs hatch in that order, too, so owlet siblings will be of
varying sizes.

The female of most owl species starts brooding, or sitting on the eggs to keep them warm, after the first egg is laid. During this period, she does not leave the nest, and the male owl has to provide food for her and for himself. The female sits on the eggs for an average of thirty days.

As with all birds, when owls breed depends on when the most food is available. The timing of the hatching usually occurs when the species' preferred prey is abundant, often soon after the prey animals give birth to their own young.

Pel's fishing owl of Africa breeds in the dry season, when low waters make it easier to spot fish. The female lays its eggs when the waters are either at their peak level or just beginning to fall. This ensures a plentiful and more easily caught food source for the hungry young.

Growing Up

By the time the last owlet hatches, the first has grown quite a bit and has the advantage of a stronger voice, which gets it more food. In abundant years, most of the owlets will survive, but many often starve. Those that do go hungry and die may be eaten by their siblings, especially if there is not much other food available. This is necessary so owls can be sure of raising one or two healthy young. In years of especially low food supplies, no owlets at all may survive the breeding season.

About three to four weeks after the first egg hatches, the mother owl can leave the nest and join the father in hunting. A brood of rapidly growing owlets requires a lot of food. When the owlets are very young, the parents bite the heads off the prey before feeding it to them. As the owlets get older, the parents will crush the heads and give the whole animals to the babies to tear up for themselves.

The length of time that it takes the young to leave the nest—the fledging period—depends on the species of owl. Great horned owls may spend as much as seventy days in the nest, while the tiny elf owl is out of the nest in only twenty-eight days. Owls that nest on the ground are active and mobile much earlier than those that nest in holes. This is because young ground-nesting owls have to be able to avoid predators. Short-eared owlets, for example, can duck into the tall grass while their parents are off finding food.

Eventually the owlets start leaving the nest, flapping their wings as they hop along tree branches. Soon they make their first attempts at flight.

Dispersal

Eurasian eagle owls' long fledging period means they have to start their breeding earlier than most species, so that the young have time to learn to fly and hunt before heading out on their own. The parent owls continue to feed and care for their young for five to six months after they leave the nest.

Eventually the time comes when the parents stop feeding the young, forcing them to fend for themselves. For migratory species, this occurs just before the owls leave for their wintering grounds.

When young owls do finally disperse, the male parent begins the whole process again—singing and checking out nesting sites for the next breeding season. Meanwhile, the young owls are out looking for territories of their own to call home. Common barn owls may travel 50 to 100 miles (80.5 to 161 km) from their parents' range before they settle down.

Although many species are sexually mature at one year of age, it may take much longer than that for them to find mates and

THESE YOUNG SPOTTED OWLS ARE WAITING NEAR THE NEST FOR THEIR PARENTS TO
RETURN WITH FOOD.

establish their own territories. Many of them never will. Fifty to 70 percent of all young owls die in their first year of life.

Predator-Prey Cycles. Just as the rise of flowering plants during the late Cretaceous Period fueled the sudden increase in the small mammal population and, consequently, the rise in predator numbers, this dynamic is still in effect today. The numbers of owls and other predators are strongly influenced by the size of their prey populations. Predators' habitat type and size, clutch

WHEN THESE BARRED OWL CHICKS ARE OLD ENOUGH, THEY WILL DISPERSE TO NEW AREAS AND SEARCH OUT TERRITORIES AND MATES OF THEIR OWN.

size, and even their physical makeup is dictated by the animals they hunt and the amount of food their home range yields.

Owls living in the boreal forest and on the tundra are particularly prone to major fluctuations in their population sizes. Snowy owls, great gray owls, and Eurasian pygmy owls feed almost exclusively on the large numbers of voles, lemmings, mice, and other rodents found in various habitats. Rodent numbers are in turn influenced by the amount of seeds produced by certain trees.

The trees have evolved this strategy in order to maintain their populations. If a tree species produced a fixed amount of seeds every year, the rodents and birds would probably eat them all. This might mean the eventual extinction of that species of tree. But by producing an occasional large crop—more seeds than the various local animals could possibly consume—the trees ensure that some seeds will germinate and grow into new trees. Bird and mammal populations cannot respond and expand quickly enough to eat all the seeds.

Norway spruce trees produce big crops of cones every three or four years. This causes songbird populations to rise as well. As the birds feed on the cones, many cones and seeds drop to the forest floor, giving rodents access to the large seed crop. The increase in food allows the rodents to breed with increased frequency, swelling their populations also.

When there is such an abundant supply of fresh meat running around, the result for owls and other predator birds is larger clutches and/or multiple clutches. When the trees produce only a small number of seeds the following year, a drastic reduction in the rodent population occurs. With no food to eat, owls stop breeding and move into areas well outside their normal habitats, expanding their search for food. While some return to their home ranges, many owls do not survive.

This same pattern occurs with other species of prey and predators. In boreal Canada, hare populations are on a ten-year boom-and-bust cycle. One of their predators, the great horned owl, mirrors that population change.

7 Hurting and Helping

Humans and owls have shared a long history, and the relationship has been at times both respectful and harmful. Depending on a particular people's cultural beliefs, an owl may be honored or persecuted. Some Australian Aboriginal tribes view owls as representing humans, while in Puerto Rico, for example, a group of coffee plantation workers in the 1800s killed owls they incorrectly believed were eating coffee beans.

Owls have also suffered as ever-increasing numbers of humans use up a dwindling supply of natural resources. The need for trees for wood products and for more farms to raise crops to feed Earth's swelling population is resulting in more and more acres of land being cleared of trees. This not only destroys owls' and many other creatures' natural habitats, it also potentially poisons their food supply because of the pesticides used on the crops.

THE PRESENCE OF BURROWING OWLS OUTSIDE AND SOMETIMES IN TOWNS AND CITIES OF THE WESTERN AND SOUTHERN UNITED STATES HAS CAUSED CLASHES BETWEEN DEVELOPERS WHO WANT TO BUILD ON THEIR HABITATS AND ENVIRONMENTALISTS AND OTHER CITIZENS WHO WANT TO SAVE THE INCREASINGLY RARE BIRD.

Humans have begun to realize the damage done to ecosystems and the wildlife that is a part of them, and some countries are taking measures to control this damage by protecting habitats. Other groups are taking more direct action by seeking to rehabilitate injured owls and return others, whose populations have been affected, to their native habitats.

Dangers to Owls

Superstitions. The long history of cultural beliefs identifying owls as omens of death and ill will have taken their toll on the real-life populations of some species. Many owls are hunted and killed because they are believed to be bad luck. Some African tribes believe that owls are evil creatures.

In some cases, even when owls were respected as powerful creatures, they were still harmed. Soups and medicines were made from owl parts in the belief that the owls' powers would be transferred to the people who ingested them. Owl eyes were eaten in the false hope that people would be able to see better at night. In ancient England, owl broth was considered a cure for whooping cough. And owl eggs were once eaten by people across Europe as a cure for drunkenness.

Snowy owls were eaten as far back as Neolithic times, and even today snowy owls and great horned owls are eaten by some native tribes in Alaska. Their feathers and feet are also used for crafts and ceremonial purposes.

Owls are also killed in areas of Asia. Medicines are made from their body parts in China and Korea. The Aino, an ancient culture of Japan, revered Blakiston's fish owl as a messenger of the gods. A ceremony that sends the owls back to the gods with messages involves capturing and killing the owls to release their spirits.

OWLS ARE OFTEN CAUGHT TO ASSESS THEIR RELATIVE HEALTH AND POPULATION SIZE
AND ARE THEN RELEASED AGAIN.

Pesticides. The increased use of agricultural pesticides after World War II caused an extremely rapid decline in the populations of many raptors. Because DDT, the first major pesticide to be widely used in North America, builds up in fatty tissues, the toxins become more concentrated as they move up the food chain from smaller animals to larger predators.

Owls and hawks are at the end of a sometimes long chain that can leave their systems poisoned and greatly damaged. Smaller doses of DDT stay in their fatty tissues. When the raptors have to tap these fat reserves, as during migration or a particularly lean hunting season, the poisons are quickly released into their bodies, resulting in an agonizing death.

DDT also affects a raptor's hormones, interfering with the movement of calcium in their bodies. This results in weakened eggshells. Many DDT-poisoned female hawks and owls crushed their thin-shelled eggs when they sat on them to brood. This inability to successfully reproduce nearly caused many raptor and other bird species to become extinct.

Other chemicals, such as dieldrin, have more immediate effects; even small doses can kill animals quickly. The reproductive systems of those that survive the initial exposure are so harmed that the animals are unable to breed.

When the world was alerted to the large decline in raptor numbers as well as to other effects of these chemicals, a movement emerged to ban them. Many industrialized nations, such as Great Britain, Canada, and the United States, eventually prohibited the use of these chemicals in the early 1970s. But many smaller, developing countries continue to use them today. As a result, large numbers of migratory birds are still affected by DDT and other chemicals because they winter in those countries.

Poorer nations often turn to chemical use as the cheapest way of ensuring that large amounts of food will be harvested for their growing populations. Farmers in those countries do not have the money and resources to come up with alternative methods for protecting crops. However, these practices cannot be used for long because the land and water are being poisoned. In addition, the soils may become depleted of nutrients, and food production may suffer.

Persecution. Raptors, including owls, have been killed over the centuries because they were considered vermin. Farmers thought, often wrongly, that owls were killing their livestock. Many owls were shot on sight.

The owners of some large estates in Europe stocked their extensive acres of woodlands with game for sport hunting. Eagle owls and other predators hunted this rich game source as well. In order to protect the game their employers had invested in, the gamekeepers killed a large number of owls and hawks. The same thing happened to the great horned owl in North America.

What these gamekeepers did not realize was that the rodent control that owls and other birds of prey provide actually benefits game species such as pheasant and grouse. When these predators are killed, rodents overrun the meadows and grasslands that the game birds prefer. The rodents consume vast amounts of seed, and, consequently, the kinds of plant species may change in response, making the habitat ultimately unsuitable for the birds.

People also hunted with owls, though they did not train the birds to hunt, as is done in falconry. Hunters used the natural response of songbirds to mob owls to capture these smaller birds in large numbers for the pet trade or to eliminate them as pests. A captured eagle owl was tied to a tree, and when the songbirds came in to mob the predator, they were caught in nets. Falconers would also use this method to capture the falcons they used for their sport, since falcons will also harass owls.

Collisions. One of the most common causes of death and injury to owls is accidents with cars and trucks. Owls, as well as other raptors, often hunt roadways because the grassy roadsides are visited by small rodents and songbirds.

The Vermont Raptor Center reported that collisions with motor vehicles accounted for approximately one-quarter— more than any other cause—of all injured birds brought to their wildlife rehabilitation center in 2003.

Barn owls in England are commonly hit by vehicles as well. This tragedy has become so widespread that taxidermy is seeing a renewed popularity. People bring the dead birds to be stuffed for display in their homes.

Habitat Destruction. Although poison, hunting, and cars may seem like potent killers of owls, none of these is as destructive to owls worldwide as the loss of their habitats.

Most owl species nest in holes in trees and consequently need large trees in which to live. They also need to be close to open areas where they can hunt. In order to make Earth more productive and to accommodate the increasing numbers of humans on the planet, more and more land has been changed from its natural state—such as forests, meadows, or wetlands— and used as sites for farms, houses, and other buildings and development. This reduces the amount of habitat available to owls and all other wildlife and plants.

Since farmland has replaced many forested areas and meadows all over the world, rodents have turned for food to the more easily obtainable supplies of grains that farmers grow and store. However, today's more advanced process of harvesting and storing grains is less wasteful and more efficient than in the previous century, leaving less lying around for rodents to clean up. Rodent populations and, thus, owl populations have declined. Both groups of animals suffer.

MORE AND MORE, OWLS AND OTHER BIRDS OF PREY ARE TURNING UP DEAD ALONG
ROADWAYS. OWLS ARE HIT BY CARS AS THEY SWOOP DOWN ON RODENTS THAT ARE
FORAGING ALONG GRASSY MEDIANS AND SHOULDERS.

Endangered Owls

The various threats to birds around the world has led in the
past to several extinctions. Some species of owls were more sensitive to human disturbance than others.

The laughing owl, related to the hawk owls, was native to
the open country of New Zealand. Although plentiful when
Europeans arrived on the islands, this species has not been seen
since 1914. A variety of factors contributed to its disappearance,

THE NORTHERN SPOTTED OWL REQUIRES LARGE AREAS OF MATURE EVERGREEN FORESTS FOR FORAGING AND NESTING. TO PROTECT THE BIRD'S HABITAT, MANY LOGGING OPERATIONS IN OLD-GROWTH FORESTS OF THE WESTERN UNITED STATES HAVE HAD TO SHUT DOWN.

including habitat destruction and overhunting. The laughing owl may not have had many natural predators, so it may not have been able to fly as well as other owls, making it more vulnerable to introduced predators, such as cats and dogs.

Many owl species are currently in danger of becoming extinct. Bird Life International, a conservation organization, lists twenty-five species of owls as endangered or vulnerable. A new owl species, the Pernambuco pygmy owl, was recently discovered in Brazil. It lives in one of the most threatened forests in the world, and as a result, the owl is already considered critically endangered.

Another owl, the mostly diurnal forest owlet, was recently rediscovered in 1997 after not being seen for more than a century. Subsequent surveys have revealed fewer than two hundred forest owlets in existence. Therefore, it is listed as critically endangered. The forests of central India where it lives are rapidly being cleared for farmland by local residents.

While the estimated population of Blakiston's fish owl is greater than the numbers of laughing owls, Pernambuco pygmy owls, or forest owlets, the species is declining due to many threats in its current habitat in Siberia, Mongolia, and Japan. The cutting of forests not only directly affects its nesting habitats in woodlands along rivers and streams, but the loss of plant cover causes soil runoff into the streams where the owls hunt, making fish more difficult to find. In Russia and Japan, fish populations have also been reduced by overfishing. Dam construction threatens to flood the owl's habitat as well. The bird has legal protection in all the countries it lives in, and some cities and towns are using nesting boxes to encourage the fish owl to breed.

Saving Them

Conservation. Owls and other wildlife need help if they are going to survive. Fortunately, a number of organizations are working to protect the habitats of these creatures. Protected lands offer places where development is prohibited and nature can run its course.

But protecting habitat is sometimes not enough. Since people need to live on and use the land as well, it is necessary to create ways to manage it for the benefit of both animals and people for centuries to come. Farmers have recognized the value of a good owl around their farms. Barn owls provide remarkably effective rodent control; they can consume around one thousand mice a year.

The northern spotted owl, an endangered subspecies of the spotted owl from the Pacific Northwest in the United States, has been at the center of controversy over the logging of mature forests in the region. Since this owl requires forests made up of large old trees, it is in direct competition with lumber companies. Many logging operations have been shut down as a result of the need to protect this species's habitat.

Although maintaining local economies is important, it is also important to keep the northern spotted owls from dying out, especially since they can act as environmental indicators of forest health. Having these owls in a forest means that the forest is healthy. If they are not present, then that particular kind of forest is changing or has already been altered.

As many as eighty-two species of owls live in older forests around the world, such as Blakiston's fish owl along river corridors in eastern Russia and the unusual bay owl in the dense evergreen forests of the Himalayas. By using the presence of these birds as an indicator of healthy forests, land managers can

Education is an important tool in the effort to save owls and other animals. This ranger in Virginia's Shenandoah National Park holds a barred owl on her glove in a demonstration for visitors.

also protect many other species of plants and animals that rely on these same forests for their survival by setting aside appropriately sized reserves.

One of the best ways to conserve owls and their habitats is to educate people about the value of these animals. Programs in schools and at nature centers, sometimes with live birds on view, help young people understand the role that owls play in the natural world. In order to make people more aware of owls, some countries have created stamps featuring them.

Owl Rearing. In some places where populations of certain owl species have become locally extinct, there have been successful efforts to reintroduce birds raised in captivity to their native habitats.

One method is called captive breeding. Researchers work to breed owls and either use their healthy eggs to replace unhealthy ones in wild owl nests, or the scientists raise the chicks themselves, releasing them into the wild when the birds are old enough to take care of themselves.

Eurasian pygmy owls were once common in Germany's Black Forest. When the forests were harvested after World War II, the pygmy owl population dropped sharply because the owls depended on those forests for nesting and hunting. Another species, the tawny owl, increased its already large population in response to the cutting and the decline of the pygmy owls because it can thrive in more varied habitats. Tawny owls also preyed upon the smaller pygmy owls.

Later, when the forests were replanted, the tawny owl population dropped. In the 1960s, researchers were able to release in the Black Forest pygmy owls that had been bred in captivity. Today there is a healthy pygmy owl population once again living

ELF OWLS IN THE DESERTS OF THE AMERICAN SOUTHWEST ARE NORMALLY DEPEND-
ENT ON WOODPECKER HOLES IN TREES AND SAGUARO CACTI FOR NESTING SITES, BUT
THEY WILL USE NESTING BOXES IF THOSE SITES ARE NOT AVAILABLE.

in that forest. And the tawny owl still survives in healthy numbers in other habitats in Europe.

In areas where suitable nesting sites are limited because large trees have been removed, people sometimes put up nesting boxes for owls. Many species use these boxes willingly, and this practice has helped some species to recover.

A subspecies of burrowing owl in Florida is being aided by new homeowners in the Marco area who allow the owls to nest on their properties. Some people have even started burrows for them, which the owls have expanded and used as nesting sites. The residents like having the owls around, not only because they are interested in the species and its welfare, but also because they receive the added benefit of the insect control that the owls provide.

The Future of Owls

In the twenty-first century, humans, in spite of all their scientific advances, seem to be just beginning to understand how ecosystems function and how wildlife—plants, animals, and all the other many forms of life—fit into these systems.

Owls inhabit the dreamlike and hidden world of night and, consequently, have remained more mysterious than other creatures. Their role as predators—and extremely quiet and efficient ones at that—has caused owls to be maligned and feared as well as respected and revered, giving rise to many myths. Now that we are beginning to understand their vital roles, from the snowy owl population's balancing act with the lemmings of the tundra to the little owl's farmer-friendly appetite for insects, perhaps we will learn that these overseers of the twilight realm need healthy habitats in order to live and grow, just like every creature on the planet. We need to save some space for them too.

Glossary

barbs—the many small, thin parts attached to a shaft that make up a bird's feather

boreal forest—a forest of the far north, made up mostly of coniferous trees

clutch—a group of eggs laid by one female and kept warm and protected by both males and females

coniferous—referring to woody plants that retain their leaves, such as pine, spruce, and fir trees, which have needlelike leaves, and many tropical plants, which have broad, flat leaves

deciduous—referring to woody plants that shed their leaves in response to seasonal changes, such as cold or drought; these plants occur most commonly in temperate regions

dispersal—the act of leaving one territory for another; generally when young birds leave their parents' care and seek out their own territories

diurnal—active during daylight hours

ecosystem—a community of plants and animals interacting with its environment

evolution—the long-term process of a species changing into a new form in order to adapt to new environmental conditions

family—a level of classification of living things that includes a group of genera; examples include the family Tytonidae (barn owls) and the family Strigidae (true owls) within the order Strigiformes

fossil—the impression of the remains of a living plant or animal left in the earth's crust

genus—a group of species; examples include wood owls, known by their Latin genus name *Strix*

gizzard—the muscular pouch behind a bird's stomach that grinds the food into digestible matter

glandular stomach—the first part of a bird's stomach that softens the food with acids and enzymes before passing it to the gizzard

habitat—the environment or natural community of plants and animals where a particular species lives

mammal—a warm-blooded animal, such as a mouse, a wolf, or a human

nocturnal—active at night

order—a level of classification of living things that includes a group of families; for example, the Strigiformes order is made up of two owl families, Tytonidae and Strigidae

predator—an animal, such as an owl, that preys upon and eats other animals, such as mice

prey—an animal that is hunted for food

raptor—a bird of prey, such as a hawk, an eagle, or an owl

species—the finest level of classification of living things; identifies a particular organism, such as the barred owl, known by its Latin species name, **Strix varia**

trait—a distinguishing feature of an organism, such as an owl's facial disk or predatory behavior

Species Checklist

This is a list of all the owls discussed in this book. For a more thorough list of the 212 species of owls in 26 genera in the world, please refer to König's *Owls: A Guide to Owls of the World* or to http://www.owlpages.com on the Internet.

	Common Name	Scientific Species Name
Order Strigiformes **Family Tytonidae** BARN, BAY, AND GRASS OWLS	African grass owl Asian bay owl Common barn owl	*Tyto capensis* *Phodilus badius* *Tyto alba*
Family Strigidae (True Owls) SCREECH AND SCOPS OWLS	Common scops owl Eastern screech owl Western screech owl	*Otus scops* *Megascops asio* *Megascops kennicotti*
EAGLE OWLS	Blakiston's fish owl Eurasian eagle owl Fraser's eagle owl Great horned owl Mackinder's eagle owl Pel's fishing owl Snowy owl	*Bubo blakistoni* *Bubo bubo* *Bubo poensis* *Bubo virginianus* *Bubo capensis mackinderi* *Scotopelia peli* *Bubo scandiacus*
WOOD AND SPECTACLED OWLS	Barred owl Eurasian tawny owl Great gray owl Spectacled owl Spotted owl	*Strix varia* *Strix aluco* *Strix nebulosa* *Pulsatrix perspicillata* *Strix occidentalis*
PYGMY OWLS	Andean pygmy owl Eurasian pygmy owl Pearl-spotted owlet Pernambuco pygmy owl	*Glaucidium jardinii* *Glaucidium passerinum* *Glaucidium perlatum* *Glaucidium mooreorum*

	Common Name	**Scientific Species Name**
ELF OWL	Elf owl	*Micrathene whitneyi*
LITTLE OWLS	Burrowing owl Forest owlet Little owl	*Athene cunicularia* *Heteroglanx blewitti* *Athene noctua*
FOREST OWLS	Boreal (Tengmalm's) owl Northern saw-whet owl	*Aegolius funereus* *Aegolius acadicus*
HAWK OWLS	Barking owl Boobook owl Laughing owl Madagascar hawk owl Morepork owl Northern hawk owl Philippine hawk owl Powerful owl	*Ninox connivens* *Ninox boobook* *Sceloglaux albifacies* *Ninox superciliaris* *Ninox novaeseelandiae* *Surnia ulula* *Ninox philippensis* *Ninox strenua*
EARED OWLS	Abyssinian long-eared owl African marsh owl Long-eared owl Madagascar long-eared owl Short-eared owl Striped owl Stygian owl	*Asio abyssinicus* *Asio capensis* *Asio otus* *Asio madagascariensis* *Asio flammeus* *Pseudoscops clamator* *Asio stygius*

Further Research

Books

Hammerslough, Jane. *Owl Puke: Book and Owl Pellet*. New York: Workman, 2003.

Heinrich, Bernd. *One Man's Owl*. Princeton, NJ: Princeton University Press, 1993.

Mowat, Farley. *Owls in the Family*. New York: Yearling Books, 1996.

Web Sites

http://www.hungryowl.org

The Hungry Owl Project, an organization dedicated to promoting the use of owls as natural predators as an alternative to pesticides and other harmful agricultural and horticultural chemicals. This site also includes information on building nesting boxes.

http://www.owlpages.com

This Web site provides a wealth of information on owls, from anatomy and natural history to species lists, plans for nesting boxes, a photo gallery, and sound files of owl calls.

http://www.vinsweb.org/raptor-center/index.html

The Web site for the Vermont Institute of Natural Science's Raptor Center, a wildlife rehabilitation and public education center.

Bibliography

Bird Life International. http://www.birdlife.org.uk/index.html, 2004.

Burton, John A. Owls of the World. New York: E. P. Dutton, 1973.

Johnsgard, Paul A. *North American Owls.* Washington, D.C.: Smithsonian Institution Press, 1988.

König, Claus, Friedhelm Weick, and Jan-Hendrik Becking. *Owls: A Guide to Owls of the World.* New Haven, CT: Yale University Press, 1999.

Leland, Charles G. *The Algonquin Legends of New England (1884).* Internet Sacred Text Archive, http://www.sacred-texts.com/index.htm, 2004.

Owl Pages, The. http://www.owlpages.com, 2004.

Sparks, John, and Tony Soper. *Owls: Their Natural and Unnatural History.* New York: Facts on File, 1989.

Sutton, Patricia, and Clay Sutton. *How to Spot an Owl.* Shelburne, VT: Chapters Publishing, 1994.

Index

Page numbers in **boldface** are illustrations.

About the Author

Tom Warhol is a photographer, writer, and naturalist from Massachusetts, where he lives with his wife, their dog, and their two cats. Tom holds both a BFA in photography and an MS in forest ecology.

Tom has worked for The Nature Conservancy, managing nature preserves; The American Chestnut Foundation, helping to grow blight-resistant American chestnut trees; and the Massachusetts Riverways Program, helping to protect and restore rivers. He has also volunteered for the Vermont Raptor Center, caring for sick, injured, and resident hawks, eagles, and owls.

In addition to *Owls*, Tom has written two other AnimalWays titles about birds of prey—*Hawks* and *Eagles*—as well as the series Biomes of Earth, also for Benchmark Books. You can see his landscape, nature, and wildlife photographs in exhibitions, in publications, and on his Web site, www.tomwarhol.com.